CHISWICK HOUSE AND GARDENS

LONDON

Roger White

Chiswick House, built between 1726 and 1729, is one of the earliest and most important neo-Palladian villas in England. Designed by Richard Boyle, third Earl of Burlington, with advice from his protégé, the painter, architect and garden designer William Kent, Chiswick House provided an exquisite setting for Burlington's collection of paintings and architectural drawings, and for highly select gatherings of his family, friends and cultural circle.

For the first few years Burlington's villa stood alongside the old Jacobean house purchased by his grandfather in 1682. This separation soon proved impractical, and in about 1732 a two-storey link was added. After the earl's death in 1753 the estate passed by marriage to the Dukes of Devonshire, and in 1788 the fifth Duke decided to demolish Old Chiswick House and make a proper mansion of the villa by adding substantial wings. Both the fifth and sixth Dukes remodelled Burlington's gardens. From the 1860s onwards the Devonshires let the house and gradually moved the historic contents to Chatsworth House, where many items remain today. In 1929 the reduced estate was sold to Middlesex County Council. In 1948, ownership of the house passed to the Ministry of Works, which embarked on a restoration campaign aimed at returning the villa to its original size and design, and the gardens to their original layout. The house and the garden buildings are now in the care of English Heritage, while the grounds are in the care of the Borough of Hounslow.

❖ CONTENTS ❖

3	TOUR OF THE HOUSE
3	*Video Room and Exhibition*
3	*Library*
4	*Lower Tribune*
5	*Ground Floor of the Link Building*
5	*Summer Parlour*
6	*Staircase*
6	*First Floor*
8	*Tribunal or Saloon*
10	*Gallery*
12	*Red Velvet Room*
14	*Blue Velvet Room*
16	*Green Velvet Room*
17	*Bedchamber and Closet*
18	*First Floor of the Link Building*
19	TOUR OF THE GARDENS
19	*Villa and Forecourt*
21	*Lawns to the West of the House*
21	*North Front of the House*
22	*Bird's-eye View of the Site*
24	*Exedra*
25	*Inigo Jones Gateway*

25	*Italian Garden and Conservatory*
26	*Deer House*
26	*Doric Column*
26	*Napoleon's Walk and Rustic House*
27	*'Patte d'oie'*
28	*Orange Tree Garden and Ionic Temple*
29	*Stone Bridge and Lake*
29	*Obelisk and 'patte d'oie'*
30	*Cascade*
31	A HISTORY OF CHISWICK HOUSE
32	*Burlington's Formative Years*
35	*Early Work at Chiswick*
36	*The Construction of the New House*
38	*The Purpose of Chiswick*
41	*The End of an Era*
42	*Chiswick under the fifth Duke of Devonshire*
43	*Chiswick under the sixth Duke of Devonshire*
43	*Chiswick in the Late Nineteenth Century*
44	*Recent History*
44	FURTHER READING
45	PLAN OF CHISWICK HOUSE

Acknowledgements
In writing this guide to Chiswick I have inevitably drawn heavily on the previous guidebook by Richard Hewlings, but I have also tried to synthesise information from other sources, notably John Harris's The Palladian Revival *and Jane Clark's various writings on the masonic and Jacobite issues. I am grateful to these three authors for their advice and help, to Julius Bryant, Julia Findlater, Cathy Power, Treve Rosoman and Juliet West of English Heritage for their comments, and to Edward Fawcett, who has a long association with Chiswick and an unsurpassed knowledge of the gardens.*

Published by English Heritage, 1 Waterhouse Square, 138-142 Holborn, London EC1N 2ST
Visit our website at **www.english-heritage.org.uk**
Chiswick House, Burlington Lane, Chiswick, London W4 2RD
Telephone: 020-8995 0508
Edited by Susannah Lawson. Designed by Pauline Hull
Printed in England by Park Communications Ltd.
© English Heritage 2001 First published by English Heritage 2001, reprinted 2003, 2007, 2010
ISBN 978 1 850 74 788 8 09465 C45 06/10
Photographs by English Heritage Photographic Unit and copyright of English Heritage, unless otherwise stated.
Works from the Devonshire Collection, Chatsworth, are reproduced by permission of the Duke of Devonshire and the Chatsworth Settlement Trustees

TOUR OF THE HOUSE

The plan on page 45 will help you to find your way round the house.

From the entrance and shop, walk down the passage to the large octagonal room at the centre of the building, known as the Lower Tribune.

To the left is a room divided into three by sets of square arches, currently used as exhibition space, and beyond that a room now containing a video on Chiswick.

Video Room and Exhibition

These rooms are modestly enriched with carved ornament and in 1770 functioned as bedrooms, with three four-poster beds. It is not known, however, whether Burlington himself ever slept here, although his wife certainly used one of the first-floor rooms as a bedroom, probably after his death.

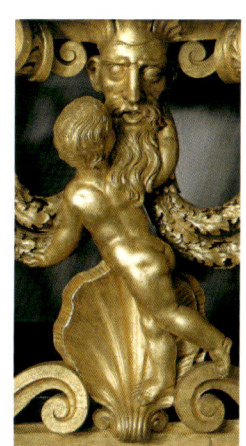

Library

The three interconnecting rooms along the north side of the ground floor were used by Burlington as his library, with bookcases specially designed by William Kent (now at Chatsworth). These rooms are likely to have contained the various books dedicated to the earl (no less than thirty-nine between 1707 and 1751), and numerous editions of all the leading Italian and French treatises on architecture, as well as many books on Roman antiquities. The exhibition now on view here includes (in the small octagonal room) an early nineteenth-century marble bust of Napoleon, possibly installed in the Rustic House in the garden by Georgiana, wife of the fifth Duke of Devonshire, and her friend the politician Charles James Fox, who were great admirers of the French emperor.

Detail of one of the giltwood side tables in the Gallery, recently returned to Chiswick

❖ RESTORING CHISWICK HOUSE ❖

Restoring Chiswick has been a challenge, not only because of its unique design, but also because of the later remodelling of the house and gardens. Moreover, the earliest inventory of contents dates from 1770, seventeen years after Burlington's death, so it can never be known with absolute certainty how the rooms were furnished in his time. Once the wings were added in 1788 the house began to be used for normal occupation, rather than as an aesthetically perfect appendage to Old Chiswick House, and the sparse look favoured by the Palladians will have changed as more up-to-date items were added. It seems likely that Burlington's furniture remained in place, augmented with later pieces, until the 1860s when the Devonshire family took the decision to let Chiswick to tenants and began to move the original furnishings to Chatsworth.

The demolition of the wings in 1956–7 was part of a plan to return the house as nearly as possible to its state under Lord Burlington, except of course that it was impossible to recreate the old house to which the villa had been attached in his time. It has also been impossible to recover all but a few of the original items of furniture, although one of the paintings from Burlington's collection has been returned on loan from Chatsworth. The policy since 1957 has therefore been to bid for original items that come on the open market, such as the pair of side tables in the Gallery, and to add furniture and paintings of a similar type and period. This approach is complicated by the fact that the furniture specifically designed for Chiswick in the 1720s and 1730s tends to be scaled down to suit the small size of the rooms, so that normal chairs and tables often look too large. There is also a phased programme to restore the decoration of individual rooms to their original condition, as revealed by paint and textile research. The Blue Velvet Room benefited from this treatment in 1991, and the Tribunal in 1996.

From the corner of this room steps lead down to an octagonal basement or wine cellar, with racks supporting wine casks.

Walk back into the main library room and through to the Lower Tribune.

Lower Tribune

The main architectural feature of the Lower Tribune is a ring of eight Tuscan columns supporting the weight of the stone floor above. In 1770 it contained twenty chairs and little else, so it was probably originally used as a waiting-room for visitors wishing to see Burlington, whose private rooms lay to the north and west. To the right (east) are several very plain rooms, not open to the public, which in the eighteenth century functioned as service rooms; in 1770 one was a Butler's Pantry and another a Linen Room. There was certainly no kitchen in the villa until the addition of wings in 1788, and any food eaten here must have been prepared in the kitchen of the old house.

Retrace your steps and go back into the small octagonal library room.

Ground Floor of the Link Building

A door from the small octagonal room leads via a short corridor into the ground floor of the Link Building, added by Lord Burlington in about 1732–3 to provide a covered connection between the old Jacobean house and the new villa. At this level the interior is absolutely plain except for screens of Tuscan columns. The room is used to display several important original pieces of sculpture that have been brought in from the garden for protection. One is the Hellenistic relief of a man and woman (probably carved to record a marriage) that had formed part of the Earl of Arundel's celebrated early seventeenth-century collection of antique sculpture, and was given to the eighteen year-old Burlington in 1712 after being dug up on the site of Arundel House in the Strand. Burlington had it inserted into the base of the obelisk by the Burlington Lane Gate in about 1728. Also here is a lead sphinx, made by the sculptor John Cheere (1709–87) and installed alongside the path from the Link Building to the 'patte d'oie' in 1749. In the next room are three ancient Roman marble statues, said to have been excavated from the ruins of the Emperor Hadrian's great villa at Tivoli, south of Rome. Burlington initially kept them in the temple in the Orange Tree Garden, but in the mid-1730s moved them outside to be the focus of the Exedra. Finally, there is Richard James Wyatt's marble statue of 'a nymph preparing for the bath', carved in about 1841. Purchased by the sixth Duke, it stood for many years under the dome of the conservatory.

Continue down the corridor and turn left into the Summer Parlour.

Summer Parlour

What is now known as the Summer Parlour seems to have been built as a single-storey addition to the old Jacobean house, perhaps as early as 1716 or 1717. The design has been attributed both to Burlington and James Gibbs, who at about the same time was doing work at Burlington House. In 1735 the interior was completely redesigned by William Kent as a garden room for Lady Burlington, whose flower garden and

The ground floor of the Link Building, with John Cheere's lead sphinx

Ancient marble relief, once part of the Earl of Arundel's celebrated sculpture collection

6 ❖ Tour of the House

Detail from the ceiling of the Summer Parlour, showing the heraldic owl of the Savile family

Opposite: Plan of the Baths of Diocletian, Rome, reconstructed by Palladio and once in Burlington's collection

William Kent, *Drawing of Lady Burlington in the Summer Parlour*

aviary lay immediately to the east. The main surviving feature of the room – probably the only interior at Chiswick designed in its entirety by Kent – is the ceiling, which has deep beamed compartments decorated by Kent in a 'grotesque' style, with figures, foliage and animal forms fancifully intertwined.

Lady Burlington was a member of the Savile family, whose heraldic emblem of an owl appears in the corner panels of the ceiling. It was also incorporated in furniture specially made for the room by John Boson – a pair of mirrors and commodes which are now at Chatsworth (see page 39). These appear in the background of a sketch by Kent which shows Lady Burlington in this room. She is depicted seated on a sofa, which was part of a set of gilded furniture (two sofas and ten chairs) supplied to her by Stephen Langley at a cost of £106; five of the chairs are on display in the Green Velvet Room upstairs. The chimneypiece comes from one of the eighteenth-century wings, replacing the original by Kent which is now at Chatsworth.

Return to the main building and continue through the library rooms to the circular corner room. From here a spiral staircase leads up to the first floor. Go up the stairs and stop in the round gallery room.

Staircase

Following the example of Palladio's celebrated Villa Rotonda at Vicenza, Burlington placed small spiral staircases at the angles of his central octagon (today only one is accessible to the public). Initially he seems to have considered incorporating a normal dog-leg staircase into the entrance hall, but in the event left it out. This meant that, unless they used the grand external stairs, access between the two floors for ladies in the fashionable wide hooped skirts of the time was very difficult, as it would have been for servants carrying trays. In fact, since there was no kitchen in Burlington's villa, conventional dining (other than cold buffets) must have taken place in the old house. This apparent disdain for ordinary practicalities is rather characteristic of the man, not only in his own buildings but also in those he designed for others.

First Floor

A very important feature of the villa plan is the way in which rooms of different geometrical shapes – square, circle, rectangle, octagon – are arranged around a central octagonal hall. This had not been seen in England before, and is something which Burlington probably derived from studying two particular sources: the published plan of Palladio's Villa

WILLIAM KENT

With the help of Burlington's friendship and patronage, Kent progressed from being a second-rate painter to England's most influential architect and garden designer of the 1730s and 1740s. Although he shared Burlington's devotion to Palladio, Jones and Roman antiquity, his own buildings show a greater freedom and inventiveness, and in some cases a grasp of the theatrical gesture that has been called 'baroque', such as the staircase of No. 44 Berkeley Square. He was an exceptionally versatile designer, equally able to turn his hand to palatial country houses (for instance Holkham Hall in Norfolk), grand interiors (such as Houghton Hall, also in Norfolk), furniture, garden buildings, ladies' dresses and even a baby's pram. He was a pioneer in the revival of the Gothic style, and he played a crucial role in steering English garden design away from formality towards a more natural look, conceived as a series of landscape pictures dotted with temples and follies. The gardens at Rousham near Oxford are a good example of his work.

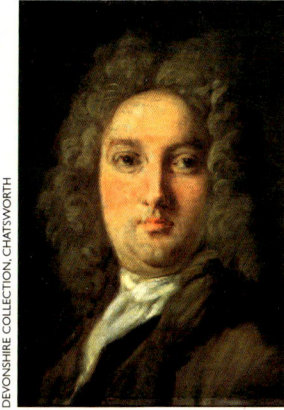

Benedetto Luti, Portrait of William Kent, *1718*

Rotonda, and Palladio's drawings of the vast bath complexes of ancient Rome (which Burlington owned and indeed kept in the villa). As in all Palladian and neo-Palladian villas, the principal rooms at Chiswick are on the first floor and are much more richly decorated than those below. As a rule, however, the owner might spend more time in the simpler ground-floor rooms, with the first-floor rooms being used mainly for entertaining visitors. In the case of Chiswick, recent research has put forward the controversial theory that some of the decorative details indicate Burlington's secret Jacobite sympathies, and the possibility that he intended the villa as a masonic meeting place.

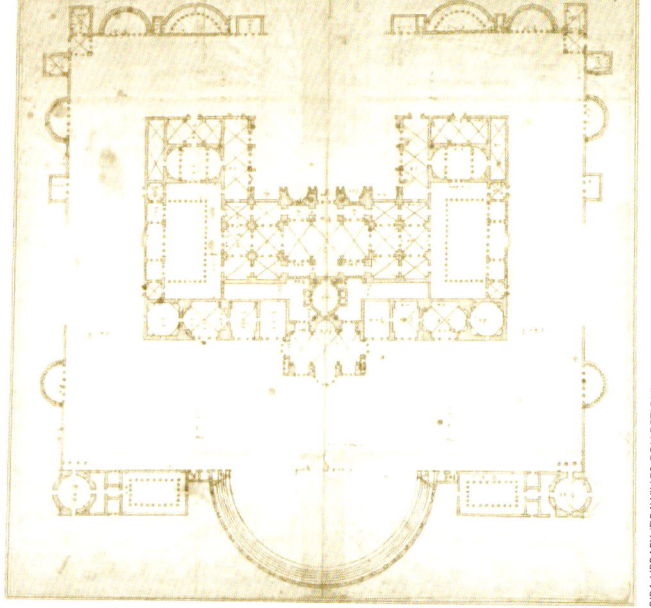

Turn right into the main gallery room and then right again into the Tribunal.

Tribunal or Saloon

The great central hall of the villa was called the 'Tribunal' by an early visitor in 1727, and the 'Salloon' in the 1770 inventory. This was the first room that visitors entered on arriving via the portico on formal occasions. Apart from its practical function as a hall from which to reach the other main rooms on this floor, and perhaps as the focal point at parties and receptions, it is primarily an imposing architectural space. With its stone floor, bare plaster walls, lofty dome and absence of any form of heating, it was certainly not a cosy space for sitting. In the eighteenth century it was furnished with four grand marble-topped gilded tables (now in the State Dining-Room at Chatsworth), each flanked by mahogany hall chairs. In the decoration there is a strong emphasis on classical antiquity: the coffering of the dome is copied from the Basilica of Maxentius in Rome, and placed around the walls on brackets are copies of Roman busts in trios (these replace the ones that were here in Burlington's time, which are now at Chatsworth).

The other main decorative element is provided by the eight large paintings that occupy the upper half of the walls. An illustration of the room published by Kent in 1727, before work on the villa was very far advanced, shows a significantly different scheme, with larger doorcases, smaller canvases and no busts. The fact that the paintings now over the doors seem to sit on top of the pediments may suggest that they were among the works of art brought from Burlington House in about 1733, and were squeezed in almost as an afterthought. With one exception, however, they have been in place since at least about 1740. Three of them represent the sort of classical themes frequently found in grand houses of the period: *The Judgement of Paris*, *Apollo and Daphne* and *The Rape of Proserpine*. Another three have Stuart connections: Louis XIII of France (Charles I's brother-in-law) and his wife Anne of Austria, and (perhaps a rather tenuous connection) the Moroccan ambassador to the Court of Charles II. Over the door to the Gallery, and facing the arriving visitor, is an early copy of Van Dyck's painting of 1632 of Charles I and his family – clearly an unequivocal Stuart subject, and potentially a statement of support for the Jacobite cause. Opposite it until 1845 hung a smaller group portrait of

Early design for the Saloon from William Kent's Designs of Inigo Jones, *1727*

Burlington and his sisters as children (now at Chatsworth). In its place hangs a large painting, *Liberality and Modesty* (a copy of an original by Guido Reni now at Althorp House), which Burlington purchased in 1743 and had in the old house at Chiswick.

Sir Godfrey Kneller, Portrait of Lord Burlington and his Sisters when Children, c.*1700, which hung in the Tribunal until 1845*

The Tribunal. The large canvases, including a copy of Van Dyck's painting of Charles I and his family, may have been brought here from Burlington House in about 1733

10 ❖ Tour of the House

Retrace your steps into the Gallery.

Gallery

The Gallery comprises three rooms which open into each other via small arches. The rooms at either end are identical in decoration except that one is octagonal and the other is round. The tripartite form is also found in the Gallery at Holkham Hall in Norfolk (begun in 1734), in whose planning Burlington was involved. Both have chimneypieces and overmantels made up from designs by Inigo Jones. This was not primarily a picture gallery, because there would have been little or no wall space in the two end rooms for hanging even small paintings. The surface is instead treated entirely architecturally, taken up with doors, window, chimneypiece, and above these a sequence of apron-shaped panels. Above this is perhaps the most distinctive feature of the small rooms: a band of gilded female heads supporting baskets, through which acanthus leaves grow – a visual embodiment of the explanation given by the Roman architect Vitruvius of how the Corinthian capital originated.

The central room of the Gallery again has no pictures (although originally there were six hung high up above the cornice), but the richness of the carved and gilded architectural ornament makes the display of conventional works of art unnecessary. The sources for the design are either from antiquity via Palladio, or from Jones. The diamond-patterned coffering of the two apses comes from the Temple of the Sun and Moon in Rome (also known as the Temple of Venus and Rome), as illustrated by Palladio in his book *I Quattro Libri,* while the compartmented ceiling, enriched with painted decoration by Kent, recalls in miniature that of Jones's magnificent Banqueting House in Whitehall. Set into the centre is a copy of a ceiling painting by Paolo Veronese (*c.*1528–88) in the Doge's Palace in Venice, depicting the Defence of Scutari of 1474. Since this was an episode in the long struggle between Christian Europe and the advancing Muslims, it has been suggested that Burlington's unusual choice of subject has a masonic motivation. The four niches were probably always intended to contain classical statues, and since at least 1761

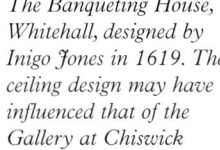

The Gallery ceiling with, inset, the copy of Veronese's The Defence of Scutari. *The other painted decoration is probably by William Kent*

The Banqueting House, Whitehall, designed by Inigo Jones in 1619. The ceiling design may have influenced that of the Gallery at Chiswick

these have been Apollo, Mercury, Venus and a Muse, all copies of antique originals. Apollo is by the eighteenth-century sculptor Peter Scheemakers; the others are modern plaster casts of pieces now at Chatsworth.

The furnishings in this room are of particular interest. Most notable, perhaps, are the two massive urns made of porphyry, which Burlington bought in Italy in 1715, and the spectacular pair of side tables. The superb inlaid marble tops may be the ones he acquired in Genoa in 1719, while the gilded wooden bases, with winged sea nymphs and cherubs standing on tiptoe in scallop shells, were probably designed by William Kent and carved by Guelfi in about 1725. The tables are likely to have been designed for this position, but left the house in the late nineteenth century when it was let to the Marquess of Bute. They found their way to Mount Stuart, the Marquess's mansion on the Isle of Bute in Scotland, from where they were bought back in 1996. The mirrors above the tables are copies of the originals, which are now at Chatsworth. In Burlington's day the room would probably have been lit by candelabra placed in front of them, and by others placed on torchère stands such as those on either side of the window (these are not original to the room). Also in the Gallery is a pair of small mahogany hall chairs, part of a set of sixteen made for Chiswick to Kent's design in about 1730. They were listed here in 1770, are shown still in place in a watercolour of 1828 (see page 43), and were bought back in 1992 and 1997. In common with the other furniture known to have been designed by Kent for Chiswick, they seem to be deliberately scaled down to match the small size of the rooms.

Like the adjoining Tribunal or Saloon, the central room of the Gallery had no heating, but in summer its Venetian door could be opened to give direct access to the gardens via the external staircase.

The Gallery, showing one of the recently returned side tables, a Kent chair and one of the porphyry urns acquired by Burlington in 1715

12 ❖ Tour of the House

William Kent, Mercury and the Arts, *a detail of the ceiling painting in the Red Velvet Room*

Right: A thistle carved on the Red Velvet Room chimneypiece

Opposite: The Red Velvet Room

Rembrandt, Portrait of an Old Man, *1651*

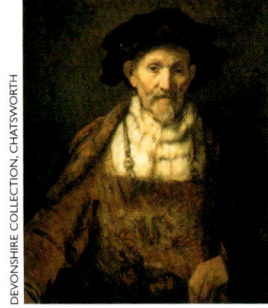

From the round gallery room, go straight on into the Red Velvet Room.

Red Velvet Room

Three of the first-floor rooms at Chiswick have always taken their names from the richly coloured velvets covering their walls – red, blue and green. Velvet was very much favoured by the English Palladians when they wanted to create a sumptuous background for hanging pictures, and often chairs would be upholstered to match. In purely architectural terms the Red Velvet Room could be seen as a homage to Inigo Jones, since the Venetian window, the beamed ceiling, the chimneypieces and their overmantels are all derived from Jones's designs. The ceiling is inset with painted panels attributed to William Kent, and has usually been interpreted as an allegory of the Arts. The panels around the edge, for instance, incorporate musical instruments, portrait roundels of gods and goddesses (Jupiter, Venus, Saturn, Mars, Diana and Apollo) and their appropriate Zodiac signs. In the central panel the messenger god Mercury hovers above a stone arch, below which is a group of figures with further emblems of the visual arts: Architecture is represented by a bare-chested woman with a set square and a cherub with a plan of a Roman temple, Sculpture by a fallen bust of Inigo Jones, and Painting by a woman unveiling a self-portrait of Kent.

The radical alternative interpretation of this symbolism is that it alludes to the ritual of the Royal Arch masonic lodge. Red is the Royal Arch colour, so the red velvet on the walls is symbolic, as is the red drape which is being removed to reveal Kent's portrait in the ceiling. The traditional implements of the architect and sculptor, depicted in the ceiling, are likewise masonic emblems, while the combination of an arch below a rainbow which occurs in the ceiling painting was apparently a common subject of early Royal Arch lodge banners. The suggestion, therefore, is that this room could have been designed by Burlington and Kent – both of whom were certainly freemasons – to function as a masonic meeting place. It is also possible that a further dimension is added by the tiny roses and thistles carved on the two chimneypieces, these being Jacobite badges that could hint at Burlington's secret political allegiance.

What is certain is that in Burlington's time the cream of his art collection was hung here, notably Rembrandt's *Portrait of an Old Man* (now at Chatsworth), together with other Dutch, Flemish and Italian paintings of the sixteenth and

TOUR OF THE HOUSE ❖ 13

14 ❖ Tour of the House

Opposite: The Blue Velvet Room

Right: The Blue Velvet Room ceiling, with painted decoration attributed to William Kent

Sixteenth-century ceiling design, the source for the Blue Velvet Room ceiling

Right: Lord Burlington's desk, now at Chatsworth House

seventeenth centuries – twenty-eight in all. The most notable works of art here today are the two overmantel paintings by Sebastiano Ricci (1659–1734). Depicting Diana and Endymion and Venus and Cupid, they are part of a set painted by Ricci for Burlington House, and were brought to Chiswick in 1729. Since the official purpose of the room was to act as an art gallery and ante-room to Burlington's study, it was sparsely furnished, with just two gilded tables and eight gilded chairs recorded here in 1770, set against the walls.

Walk through the opposite door into the Blue Velvet Room.

Blue Velvet Room

This sumptuous little room, the most richly decorated in the house, was used by Burlington as his study. The curtains and wall-coverings have been recreated to reflect their original appearance. Against the blue velvet walls were hung twenty-six small paintings, mostly Dutch landscapes. This is where privileged visitors were shown Burlington's wonderful collection of architectural drawings by Palladio, Jones and others, from which so much of the inspiration for the design of the villa had been derived. Around the walls were eight tapestry-upholstered chairs, and in the centre of the room stood Burlington's desk, now kept at Chatsworth (the desk here today was made in about 1745, possibly by Benjamin Goodison). Over the doors and windows are gilded circular frames carved with fish-tailed cherubs, inset with small portrait paintings. One of these is an early portrait of Inigo Jones (identifiable by his distinctive pointed white beard) by William Dobson (1610–46). It was first recorded in

old Chiswick House before the building of the villa, and was probably placed in this position on completion. Opening off one corner of the Blue Velvet Room is a room known as the Red Closet (not open to visitors), which is even smaller and yet in 1770 contained even more paintings.

The most striking feature of the Blue Velvet Room is the ceiling, supported on pairs of massive curving brackets, a feature which Burlington found in a sixteenth-century Italian ceiling design in his own collection. The structure is overlain with glittering decoration, predominantly in blue and gold, painted (probably by Kent) in imitation of mosaic. The central panel has usually been taken to represent Architecture, since it depicts a woman seated on a fallen column on a cloud, holding compasses and an architectural plan, and wearing a Corinthian capital rather precariously on her head. Around her are cherubs carrying drawing instruments. The alternative interpretation, however, is that because these are also masonic symbols, the room might have doubled as the setting for secret meetings of a Craft lodge (Craft masons being known as 'Blue Masons').

Go back into the Red Velvet Room and turn right into the Tribunal. The Green Velvet Room is directly opposite.

16 ❖ Tour of the House

Green Velvet Room

The Green Velvet Room matches the Red Velvet Room in shape and size, and was also used to display some of Burlington's finest paintings. It too was furnished with a few grand pieces, and here the paintings were predominantly of mythological subjects. Like the Red Velvet Room, the architectural features are all based on designs by Inigo Jones, and the gilded overmantels contain the other two paintings brought from Burlington House in about 1729: *Bacchus and Ariadne*, painted for the staircase there by Sebastiano Ricci in about 1716, and a large flower painting by Jean-Baptiste Monnoyer (1634–99), to which it is thought Ricci added the cherub to provide a visual link between the two canvases. The paintings hung on the walls today include Francesco Albani's *Mars and Venus*, which a French visitor admired here as early as 1728. Also in the room are five gilded armchairs upholstered in green velvet, part of the set originally made for Lady Burlington's Summer Parlour in 1735.

Facing the window, take the door to the right into the Bedchamber.

Bedchamber and Closet

Although there is little documentation about how the various rooms in the villa were used in Burlington's time, and no detailed inventory until 1770, it is known that Lady Burlington (who outlived her husband by five years)

died in her bed in this corner room in 1758. It is quite possible that she had her bed moved here after her husband's death. In the 1770 inventory the room is described as a bedchamber, and what is now the Green Velvet Room was 'The Lady's Dressing Room'. The bedroom must then have looked very different from now. In addition to the canopied bed with crimson-lined needlework hangings, the walls were covered with Brussels tapestries, there were two gilded sofas covered in crimson silk damask, two gilded tables with marble tops and silver hearth furniture. The small closet opening off it was furnished as Lady Burlington's private retreat, with a desk, bookcase, armchairs, table and pot cupboard. All this has long since gone, and instead there is a display of paintings (some recorded in the house in the eighteenth century), including a charming portrait by

The Bedchamber. The chimneypiece and overmantel derive from drawings by Inigo Jones

Opposite: The Green Velvet Room, with chairs made for Lady Burlington's Summer Parlour in 1735

Lady Burlington, Portrait of Lady Charlotte Boyle, c.1740

ON LOAN FROM THE DEVONSHIRE COLLECTION, CHATSWORTH

Lady Burlington of her younger daughter Charlotte, who married the future fourth Duke of Devonshire in 1748 and died only six years later at the age of twenty-three.

Return through the Green Velvet Room into the small octagonal room straight ahead and turn right through a corner door.

First floor of the Link Building, possibly used by Burlington for summer dining

Right: Drawing of a Roman ceiling, from Burlington's collection

First Floor of the Link Building

The Link Building, added in 1732 or 1733 to connect the villa with old Chiswick House and now a dead end, was primarily a glorified passage. Nevertheless, the room contained in its upper floor is, from a design point of view, one of the most interesting in the house, and more than any other evokes the spirit of Roman antiquity. The strange ceiling is closely copied from a late sixteenth-century Italian drawing, recording a now-vanished Roman ceiling at Pozzuoli near Naples. The screens of Corinthian columns with open space above (a feature subsequently much used by Robert Adam) derive from Palladio's drawings of the Baths of Caracalla in Rome. One suggestion is that this room doubled as a summer dining-room, serviced through the corridor from the kitchens in the old house. The only furnishings here at present are three monochrome panels by Sir Godfrey Kneller (1646–1723) of Apollo, Venus and Hercules, painted in about 1719 for Alexander Pope's villa up-river at Twickenham, and then left by the poet to his friend Lord Bathurst. (They have been generously lent to Chiswick House by Lord Bathurst.)

This concludes the tour of the house. Return to the ground floor via the spiral staircase from the small circular gallery room.

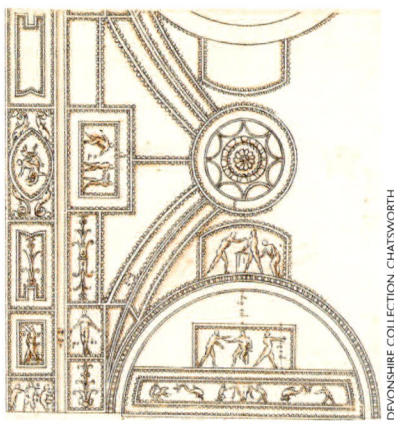

TOUR OF THE GARDENS

The bird's-eye view on page 22 will help you to find your way round the gardens.

Villa and Forecourt

In Lord Burlington's time the public road ran much closer to the house than at present, just south of the forecourt. The entrance piers were originally topped by sphinxes (now in Green Park, central London). They were possibly intended as symbolic guardians of the villa, since in classical mythology the sphinx guarded the entrance to Thebes and strangled visitors who failed to solve her riddle. Three more sphinxes are to be found in the gardens behind the house.

Jacques Rigaud, Chiswick House, the Link Building and the Old House, *1733. Notice the sphinxes on the gate piers and the public road running in front*

20 ❖ Tour of the Gardens

Vincenzo Scamozzi, The Rocca Pisani near Vicenza, a source for the design of Chiswick House

Right: Detail of the entrance front

Statues of Andrea Palladio and Inigo Jones, thought to be by the Italian sculptor Giovanni Battista Guelfi; or the Flemish sculptor John Michael Rysbrack

The forecourt is flanked by six stone pedestals ending in carved human heads, known as 'terms', set against a yew hedge. 'Terms' were used in Roman times as boundary posts (the name 'term' comes from Terminus, the Roman god who guarded over boundaries), and were frequently copied by sixteenth-century Italian architects. The Chiswick 'terms' are shown in this position in a painting of about 1728, and they were returned here in about 1950 after being moved round the grounds in 1814 by the sixth Duke of Devonshire. Jacques Rigaud's drawing of 1733, on the previous page, shows that tall spindly trees, apparently Cedars of Lebanon with their lower branches removed, were planted in front of the terms; these framed the main façade of the villa and concealed the adjoining Jacobean house (which stood immediately to the right). The existing cedars were planted in 1989.

From the forecourt the perfect proportions and exquisite carved detail of the villa's façade can be examined. Although Burlington so much admired the work of Palladio, the external form of the Chiswick villa, with its octagonal stepped dome, is in fact derived from the Rocca Pisani near Vicenza designed by Palladio's pupil Vincenzo Scamozzi (1552–1616). The capitals of the pedimented portico are copied from the ancient temple of Jupiter the Thunderer in the Roman Forum, which had been illustrated by Palladio.

It is reached by an exceptionally elaborate arrangement of steps, ornamented with elegant urns. These would have been used only on grand occasions, the normal entrance being the door to the ground floor, or rustic storey, still in use today. The two small windows tucked under the ceiling of the portico light servants' rooms. On either side of the portico are statues, thought to be by either Giovanni Battista Guelfi (fl.1713-34) or John Michael Rysbrack (1694-1770), of Burlington's two favourite architects, the patron saints of the villa as it were – Andrea Palladio on the left, and Inigo Jones on the right. Before the completion of the villa these stood outside the Bagnio, the earliest of the garden buildings.

Walk round the left-hand side of the house.

TOUR OF THE GARDENS ❖ 21

Above: Burlington's design for obelisk chimneys

Left: The west front, as restored in 1956–7

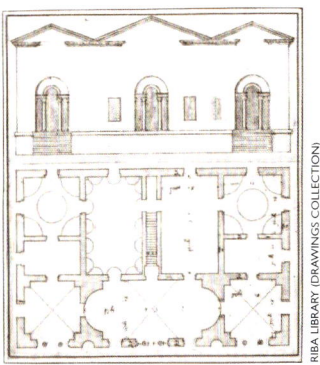

Above: Palladio's unexecuted design for a villa

Below: The north front, the Link Building and Summer Parlour

Lawns to the West of the House

When Chiswick House was first built, the western boundary of the grounds was a stream, the Bollo Brook, which Burlington later deepened and widened to create a long, narrow lake or 'river'. Between the two, what is now a sloping lawn was at first partly planted as a maze, but this was removed, possibly at William Kent's suggestion, in the mid-1730s to open up the view. Chiswick was, indeed, probably the first place in England where Kent put his new 'natural' style into practice. Further to the north was an area with a formal pool and sharply clipped hedges, reminiscent of stage 'flats'; these were cleared away when the fifth Duke of Devonshire extended the lawn in 1784. From the lawn there is a good view of the side elevation of the villa, whose main features are the tripartite central window, usually known as a 'Venetian' window, and the unusual tapering chimneys in the form of obelisks (derived from Italian Renaissance precedent). These were quickly replaced with normal chimneys because they did not work properly, but the original shape was put back as part of the 1950s restoration, when the wings added in 1788 were demolished.

Continue around the outside of the house to the north front.

North Front of the House

The north front has another elaborate staircase, connecting the Gallery on the first floor with the garden. The main features of the façade are three Venetian windows set within arched recesses, an arrangement which Burlington derived from an unexecuted design by Palladio in his own collection. At first, the façade was obscured by the Grove, a plantation of regularly and closely spaced trees. Within a year of the start of construction work on the house in 1727, Burlington – again probably with prompting from Kent –

Bird's-eye View

Orange Tree Garden
A self-contained garden which focuses on an obelisk and a small domed temple; in Burlington's time it contained numerous orange trees in tubs

Burlington Lane Gate and the 'Patte d'oie'
Created after Burlington acquired the Sutton Court estate in 1727. The obelisk incorporates a copy of an ancient carved relief

Bridge
Built by the fifth Duke of Devonshire in 1774 and probably designed by James Wyatt; the Bagnio, Burlington's first architectural design, stood nearby but was demolished in 1778

'River'
Originally a stream called the Bollo Brook, it was widened by Burlington, first into a formal canal and then into a naturalistic lake

Cascade
Designed by William Kent to terminate the view down the river, it was begun in 1738 but never worked properly in Burlington's time

Lawns West of the House
Originally divided by hedges and railings, the area was gradually opened up and deformalised under William Kent's influence

Forecourt
Framed by cedar trees and stone terms; a pair of lead sphinxes once guarded the entrance

Site of Old Chiswick House
The Jacobean mansion was demolished in 1788, when wings were added to Burlington's villa

ILLUSTRATION BY PETER DUNN

BIRD'S-EYE VIEW ❖ 23

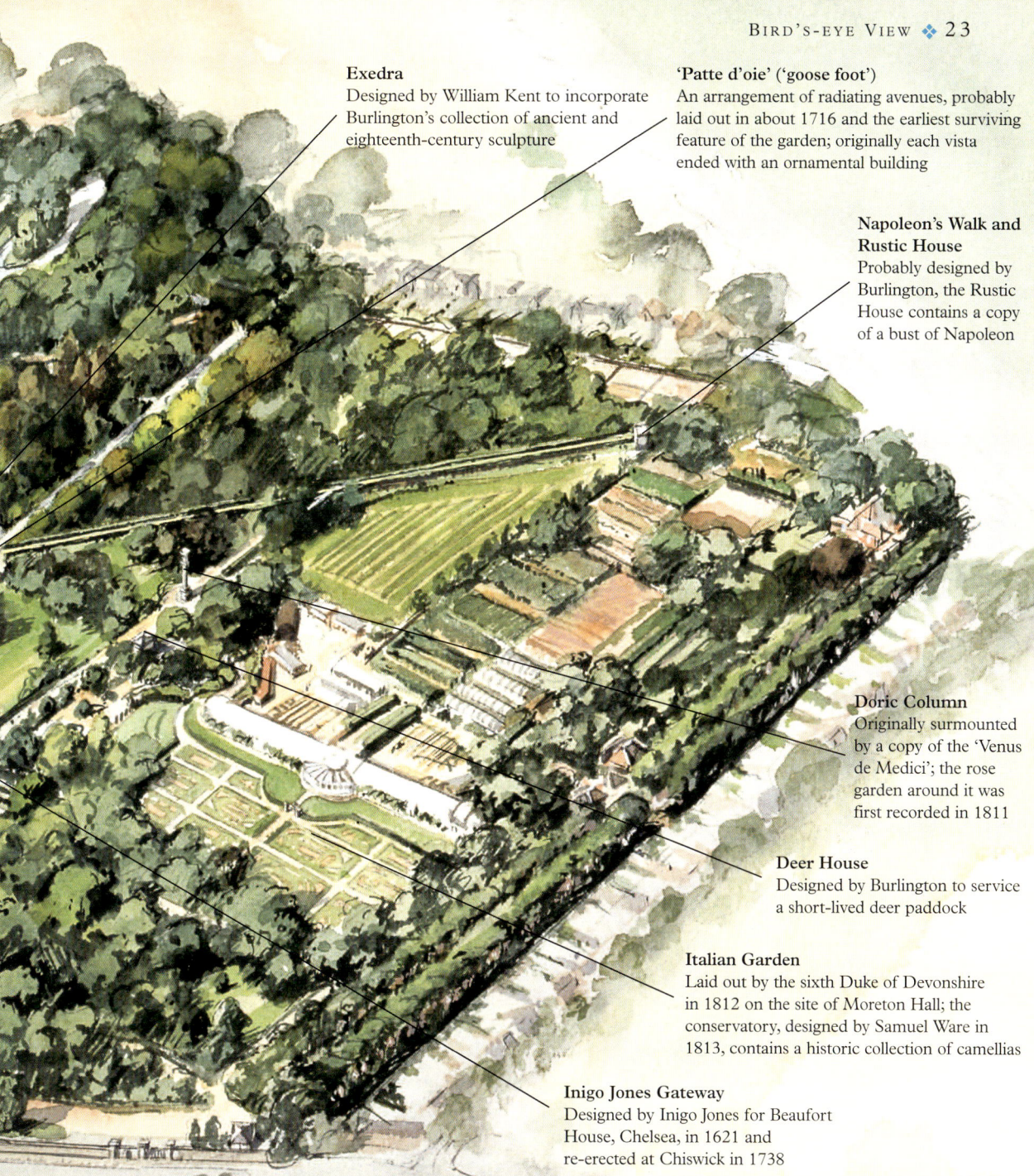

Exedra
Designed by William Kent to incorporate Burlington's collection of ancient and eighteenth-century sculpture

'Patte d'oie' ('goose foot')
An arrangement of radiating avenues, probably laid out in about 1716 and the earliest surviving feature of the garden; originally each vista ended with an ornamental building

Napoleon's Walk and Rustic House
Probably designed by Burlington, the Rustic House contains a copy of a bust of Napoleon

Doric Column
Originally surmounted by a copy of the 'Venus de Medici'; the rose garden around it was first recorded in 1811

Deer House
Designed by Burlington to service a short-lived deer paddock

Italian Garden
Laid out by the sixth Duke of Devonshire in 1812 on the site of Moreton Hall; the conservatory, designed by Samuel Ware in 1813, contains a historic collection of camellias

Inigo Jones Gateway
Designed by Inigo Jones for Beaufort House, Chelsea, in 1621 and re-erected at Chiswick in 1738

had those nearest the façade cut down to create a semicircular clearing edged with an iron railing. Rigaud's drawing of 1733 on page 40 shows the villa's immediate surroundings very much divided up by such railings and hedges. Between 1733 and 1736 more trees were removed to allow a vista northwards, the same width as the villa.

Right: William Kent, Second design for the Exedra

From this position look north across the lawn to the Exedra.

Exedra

As the 1730s progressed, Lord Burlington clearly decided to open up and unify the setting of the house, probably on the advice of William Kent. Kent had a 'pictorial' approach to garden design; unlike previous designers, he conceived gardens as semi-naturalistic pictures, similar to the paintings of such seventeenth-century artists as Claude Lorraine and Nicolas Poussin. By 1742 the western half of the Grove had been felled and a large lawn created, lined by alternating cypresses and stone urns and closed at its northern end by a semicircular hedge known as the Exedra. Although the general shape was sanctioned by presumed ancient Roman precedent (as shown by a book published in 1728 and dedicated to Burlington, Robert Castell's *Villas of the Ancients*), this feature seems to have been designed by Kent. His drawings show that it was initially intended to define the curve with a stone screen. Instead it was decided that a dark yew hedge would make a good (and cheaper) backdrop to Burlington's collection of ancient and eighteenth-century sculpture. This included three antique Roman statues which (according to Daniel Defoe in 1748) originated at Hadrian's Villa near Tivoli. They were later incorrectly said to represent Julius Caesar, Pompey and Cicero, but in fact their identity is unknown. (The statues now in the Exedra are modern copies, the originals being kept inside the house.) Also in the Exedra are more urns, flanking statues of a lion and lioness, carved

The Exedra today, with some of the sculpture shown in Kent's drawing

by Peter Scheemakers in about 1738, and a pair of 'terms' representing Socrates and Lycurgus, two ancient Greek opponents of tyranny. Whether these seemingly miscellaneous pieces of sculpture have a coherent underlying 'programme' is still debated by scholars. One theory is that together they amount to a commentary on the shortcomings of the political and moral life of Burlington's England, as contrasted with the virtues of particular figures of Greek antiquity, and possibly with those of the exiled Stuart king, James III.

Continue across the north front, passing the Link Building and Summer Parlour.

Inigo Jones Gateway

The broad path across the north front of the house passes the Link Building and Summer Parlour, and leads to a classical gateway of the Doric order. Two inscriptions on the flanking walls record that it was designed by Inigo Jones for Beaufort House, Chelsea in 1621 and donated to Lord Burlington in 1738 by Sir Hans Sloane, who was demolishing the house at the time. The gateway replaced a simpler pedimented door in a wall, no doubt designed by Burlington. This led to the deer paddock and had stood here for only a few years when the gift was made. Subsequently relocated, it now leads back to the main car park.

Passing through the gateway, go straight ahead and into the Italian Garden.

Italian Garden and Conservatory

The Jones Gateway leads from Lord Burlington's gardens into those created on the site of Moreton Hall, which the sixth Duke of Devonshire acquired in 1812. The Duke demolished the hall – a fine late seventeenth-century mansion designed by Hugh May – but kept its walled garden and the splendid iron gates that led into it. A new semicircular Italian Garden was laid out immediately to the south, with, as its backdrop, a long hothouse or conservatory designed by Samuel Ware. This was completed in 1813 with a glazed dome at its centre, the forerunner of those designed by Decimus Burton at Kew and Sir Joseph Paxton at Chatsworth. It contains an important historic collection of camellias, still largely those supplied in 1813.

The Inigo Jones gateway, designed by Jones for Beaufort House, Chelsea, 1621. It was brought to Chiswick in 1738, when the flanking walls were added

The Italian Garden, laid out for the sixth Duke of Devonshire in 1812, with the conservatory completed in 1813. The dome was rebuilt in around 1930

The Deer House, designed by Burlington to service an adjoining deer paddock

William Kent, Drawing of the Doric Column with a statue of the 'Venus de Medici'. *The Deer House is in the background*

The Italian Garden is laid out in a simplified version of the original geometrical plan by the Duke's gardener Lewis Kennedy. Stone urns are set against the enclosing curved yew hedges and the central path is flanked by copies of two magnificent urns made of Coade Stone. The original urns, now kept in the conservatory, were probably bought by the fifth Duke, and later placed in this garden by his successor. They are copies of two celebrated ancient vases: the Roman Medici Vase, decorated with the story of the Greek heroine Iphigenia, and the Greek Borghese Vase, featuring worshippers of Bacchus, god of wine.

A path to the left of the conservatory leads back into Burlington's gardens adjoining the Deer House.

Deer House

In the early stages of Lord Burlington's garden there was a paddock for deer on the eastern edge of the property, separated from the garden proper by a ha-ha (a sunken fence). At the north end of the ha-ha was a small pavilion or deer house, designed by the earl himself. After his purchase in 1727 of Sutton Court, to the west of the Bollo Brook, he made a deer park there and had the original paddock converted into a second orange tree garden. William Kent prepared a scheme which shows hedges stepping back, rather like a stage set, to a central orangery. This was built to Burlington's design, but disappeared in the nineteenth century.

Doric Column

Just to the north of the Deer House stands a tall Doric column, first recorded in a painting of about 1728 when it was crowned by a copy of the famous statue of the Venus de Medici from the Uffizi Gallery in Florence. By 1736 it was the focus of a small triangular area of dense planting, with six straight paths or 'allées' radiating out from it. This seems to have been replaced by a rose garden, laid out by the fifth Duke of Devonshire and first recorded in 1811. It has recently been replanted, having been grassed over in the 1950s.

From the column take the path to the left, which leads into Napoleon's Walk.

Napoleon's Walk and Rustic House

This long, straight path or 'allée' forms the right-hand arm of the 'patte d'oie' (see page 27). The vista to the right ends with the Rustic House, an arched alcove probably designed by Burlington and so-called not because it is particularly rustic in the sense of countrified, but because its façade is heavily ornamented with carved stonework known as rustication. It contains a copy of an early nineteenth-century bust of Napoleon (the original is kept on the ground floor of the villa), which gives its name to the walk. It was first recorded in this position in 1845, but it may have been installed some forty years earlier by Duchess Georgiana (wife of the fifth Duke) and her friend the politician Charles James Fox (leader of the Whig party), who were great admirers of the French emperor even though Britain was then at war with him.

'Patte d'oie'

Between the Doric column and the Exedra lies the fulcrum of the so-called 'patte d'oie' (French for 'goose foot'), an arrangement of three radiating avenues which is one of the key features of Lord Burlington's garden. The central avenue continues the line of what was the central path through the Grove, and before that was the main axis of the gardens of the Jacobean house. Such 'pattes d'oie' were not uncommon in late seventeenth- and early eighteenth-century formal gardens. Indeed, much grander examples were laid out for King Charles II at St James's Park and Hampton Court in the 1660s. However, the importance of Burlington's 'patte d'oie' is that, soon after it was laid out and perhaps for the first time in garden history, he took the decision to terminate each vista with an ornamental building. There may have been a theatrical inspiration for this, since Burlington was a keen patron of Italian opera in England, and had visited Palladio's Teatro Olimpico in Vicenza in 1715. The left-hand avenue was originally focused on a building called the Bagnio (bath-house) or Casina (little house), which was designed by Burlington in 1717 and was called by the Palladian architect Colen Campbell 'the First Essay of his Lordship's happy invention'. This probably gives a date of 1716 for the 'patte d'oie' as a whole, in which case it predates the building of the villa by a decade. The central avenue ended at a domed Pagan Temple, or Pantheon, completed in 1719 and often attributed to the architect James Gibbs. The right-hand avenue was terminated by

The Rustic House at the end of Napoleon's Walk

Pieter Andreas Rysbrack, A View of the 'Patte d'oie' with the Bagnio and the Domed Building, c.1728–9

the Rustic House. The completed layout is recorded in paintings made by Pieter Andreas Rysbrack in about 1728, which indicate that the outer avenues were defined by tall clipped yew hedges, while the central one had an inner avenue of regularly spaced lime trees.

Burlington had the area in between the avenues planted up with trees and shrubs to form a 'Wilderness', threaded by winding paths that linked glades and a bowling green (this still survives, edged with large sweet chestnut trees). This arrangement was thought to reproduce the kind of layout found in ancient Roman gardens, as described by the Roman author Pliny the Younger. Later in the eighteenth century the fifth Duke of Devonshire instigated changes designed to deformalise this area of the gardens, planting out the western and central avenues and demolishing their terminal buildings, in 1778 and 1784 respectively. Only the eastern avenue and the Rustic House were allowed to remain. The present arrangement is a laudable but not entirely accurate attempt of 1951–2 to return the 'patte d'oie' to its original appearance. The vanished Bagnio could not be rebuilt, however, and the place of the Pantheon was taken by a Venetian window saved from the demolition of the villa's late eighteenth-century wings.

Take the left-hand arm of the 'patte d'oie'.

Orange Tree Garden and Ionic Temple

Opening off to the left of the avenue is the enclosed area known as the Orange Tree Garden. This seems to be an addition made by 1727, squeezed into a wedge-shaped site between now-vanished formal pools alongside the Bollo Brook. It is roughly circular in form with grass terraces stepping down to a circular pool with an obelisk

Above: The Ionic Temple and obelisk in the Orange Tree Garden

Right: Pieter Andreas Rysbrack, The Orange Tree Garden, *c.1728–9, showing the original arrangement with orange trees in tubs*

at its centre. On the far side of the pool is a small temple like a miniaturised version of the Pantheon in Rome. It was designed by Burlington himself, and it housed his three Roman statues until they were moved to the Exedra.

This self-contained garden is therefore full of references to antiquity, and the stepped terraces are reminiscent of a Roman theatre. The name of the garden derives from the fact that in Burlington's time numerous orange trees in tubs were set out on the terraces in summer. Rysbrack's painting of about 1729 shows how this arrangement looked.

Continue down the avenue to the Stone Bridge.

Stone Bridge and Lake

The left-hand arm of the 'patte d'oie' originally aligned on the Bagnio, which was demolished in 1778. When it was replanted in 1951–2 the avenue was realigned slightly to the west to lead to the elegant stone bridge built by the fifth Duke of Devonshire in 1774. The bridge replaced a wooden predecessor, and its design is usually attributed to the architect James Wyatt. It spans the long, narrow 'river' which Burlington had created out of the Bollo Brook after his acquisition of the neighbouring Sutton Court estate in 1727.

Cross the bridge and take the central avenue leading to the obelisk.

Obelisk and 'Patte d'oie'

When the Sutton Court estate was incorporated into the Chiswick grounds, part of the land was used for a new deer park, and part was treated as an extension of the gardens. Everything was framed around two further interlocking 'pattes d'oie', one of them radiating out from the west end of a newly built wooden bridge and the other from a circular clearing just inside a new gate onto what is now Burlington Lane. The two 'pattes d'oie' have in common the avenue connecting the bridge with the gate, which has recently been restored to its correct appearance, with parallel rows of lime trees in front of yew hedges, and a central path of hoggin (a compound of gravel and clay which occurs naturally in the Thames Valley and was much used for this purpose in the eighteenth century). Just inside the gate, forming the fulcrum of the second 'patte d'oie', is an obelisk. Built into its base is an ancient Hellenistic carved relief of a man and woman (replaced by a copy in 1988), which had been given to the young Burlington in 1712 but had once belonged to Inigo Jones's patron the Earl of Arundel – part of the first collection of antique sculpture ever assembled in England.

The central arm of this 'patte d'oie' was made to align on the rear elevation of the temple in the Orange Tree Garden, on the far side of the lake.

The Stone Bridge, built for the fifth Duke of Devonshire in 1774, and probably designed by James Wyatt

William Kent, View of the Obelisk and Burlington Lane Gate

30 ❖ Tour of the Gardens

Right: William Kent, Design for a Cascade at Chiswick

The Cascade, as restored in 1996–7

George Lambert and William Hogarth (attrib.), View from the Cascade Terrace, c.1742

Since there was originally no door on this elevation, Burlington added a prominent pedimented porch to create a more interesting termination.

Take the right-hand avenue leading from the obelisk 'patte d'oie'.

Cascade

The right-hand arm of this 'patte d'oie' served as a carriage drive leading to a watersplash across the bottom end of the 'river'. To screen the drive from the public road close by, and to give views out across the water meadows to the Thames, Burlington had an earth bank raised, with a terrace along the top. Although such terraces were not new in gardens, Burlington set a precedent by having the banks planted up like a shrubbery, with roses and honeysuckles along the south face.

At the southern end of the 'river' Burlington soon decided to create an artificial cascade alongside the watersplash, set into the end of the terrace and closing the view to the south in a more interesting way. A number of design sketches by William Kent survive which show that various options were considered before a naturalistic rocky structure with three arches was decided upon, inspired by examples that both men had seen in Italian Renaissance gardens. The design seems to have been settled by 1736, when it was included in Rocque's illustrated map of the garden, but its construction evidently caused problems. It was not begun until 1738, and was still under way in 1744. Two years later an engineer was paid for his efforts in trying to get the cascade to work, and in 1748 the hydraulics were pronounced a failure. It remained dry and neglected until modern technology made restoration, in the spirit of the original, possible in 1996–7.

From the cascade the path leads back to the entrance to the villa forecourt.

A HISTORY OF CHISWICK HOUSE

The history of the house and grounds at Chiswick is exceptionally complex. In order to understand their evolution it is necessary to begin by looking briefly at the earlier history of the site.

When this modest estate was bought in 1682 by Lord Burlington's grandfather, the first earl, it centred on a courtyard house with typical Jacobean shaped gables, said to have been built around 1610. The only known view of this house before Burlington began work on his new villa is an engraving of around 1698–9, which shows it set back slightly from the public road. Immediately alongside is the handsome L-shaped stable range added by the first earl and not

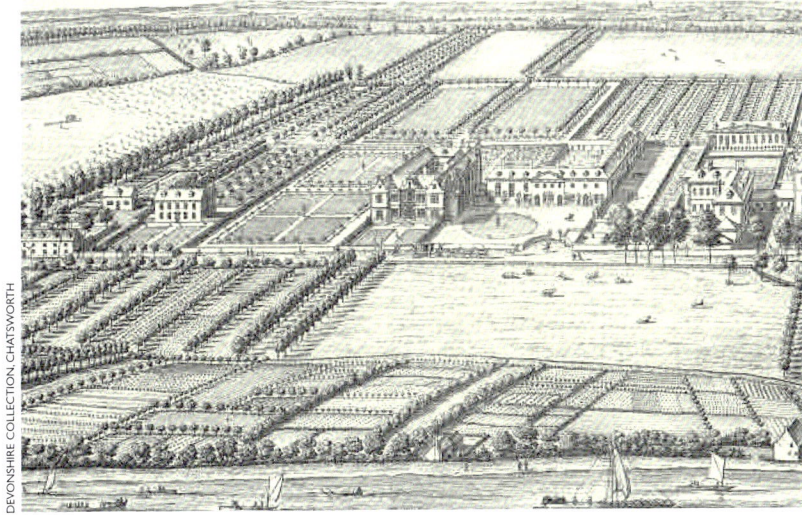

Kip and Knyff, Engraving of Old Chiswick House, *1698–9. To the right are the seventeenth-century stables, demolished in the 1920s, and beyond them the grounds of Moreton Hall, added to those of Chiswick House in 1812*

LORD BURLINGTON ❖ AND THE ARTS ❖

Although many eighteenth-century English gentlemen took an active interest in architecture and even dabbled in design, it was very unusual for an aristocrat of Burlington's status to be responsible for the design of substantial buildings. Over twenty projects are reliably attributed to him, including a number of houses for his friends and several public buildings, notably the dormitory at Westminster School (1722) and the Assembly Rooms at York (1731). A French visitor to Chiswick in 1728 noted that the earl had his drawing office in the Bagnio in the garden, although he certainly employed a succession of professional draughtsmen to turn his designs into fully finished drawings. Henry Flitcroft, for instance (nicknamed 'Burlington Harry' by contemporaries), produced most of the final drawings for Chiswick House.

William Kent, Portrait of Alexander Pope, 1735

Architecture was Burlington's passion, but his keen interest in the other arts showed itself in the creative personalities he gathered about him at Burlington House and Chiswick, or supported with financial and practical help. He subsidised publications by a considerable number of architects, poets and authors, among them William Kent, Isaac Ware, Alexander Pope, James Thomson and John Gay (author of *The Beggar's Opera*). The earl was also a notable art collector, and acquired many paintings on his Grand Tour to Italy in 1714–15. A list of his collection made in 1753 includes works by artists such as Leonardo, Titian, Domenichino and Veronese, as well as Dutch and Flemish paintings by Rembrandt, Rubens, Bruegel and others. In addition to buying Old Masters, he commissioned living artists to adorn his houses and to record the evolving gardens at Chiswick.

demolished until the 1920s. The surrounding gardens appear largely divided up into formal rectangles by rows of trees. It was these gardens that the young third earl began to remodel from about 1714 or 1715, while the continuing presence of the old house until its eventual demolition in 1788 was to have a significant effect on the way his new villa was designed and used.

Burlington's Formative Years

Richard Boyle was born in 1694 and was a boy of only ten when he inherited his father's titles and estates. These included not only the house at Chiswick and a fine town mansion in Piccadilly (today the home of the Royal Academy of Arts), but also extensive lands in Yorkshire and southern Ireland (one of his titles was fourth Earl of Cork). He must have acquired an early love of the arts, because already in 1714 he was being praised in print for his taste in gardening and painting. In May that year, like many other young English noblemen of his day, Burlington set off for Italy on his first 'Grand Tour', travelling through the Low Countries and the Rhineland and spending four months in Rome. For cultural acquisitiveness he proved to be in a class of his own, arriving home in April 1715 accompanied by not only 878 trunks of purchases (including many paintings and the two porphyry urns now in the Gallery) but also the sculptor Giovanni Battista Guelfi and the violinist Pietro Castrucci.

At this stage Burlington seems to have been more interested in music and the theatre than architecture. George Frederick Handel came to stay at Burlington House in 1713, when his host was only eighteen, and after Burlington's return from Italy took up residence for at least two years. The earl was the principal financial backer of the short-lived Royal Academy of Music, set up under the patronage of George I in 1719, and the creative artists whom he supported individually included not just musicians but writers, poets, philosophers, painters, sculptors and architects. No wonder the poet John Gay could claim that 'Burlington's beloved by ev'ry Muse'.

An interest in architecture, which was to become his ruling passion, seems to have been stirred by the publication in 1715 of two important volumes. The first was the first English translation of *The Four Books of Architecture (I Quattro libri dell'architettura)* by the sixteenth-century Venetian architect Andrea Palladio. The second was Volume I of *Vitruvius Britannicus*, a compendium of British classical architecture compiled by the Scottish architect Colen Campbell (1676–1729). Although Campbell included designs by almost all the leading British architects of the day, most of whom were still working in a baroque idiom, he made it clear that he particularly admired Palladio and his early seventeenth-century English disciple, Inigo Jones. Campbell became the young earl's first architectural mentor, and when in 1717 Burlington tried his hand at designing a building for the first time, the result – a garden pavilion at Chiswick known as the Bagnio – was very much in Campbell's style.

In 1719, with Campbell already at work transforming Burlington House in Piccadilly for him, he set off again for Italy. This time his visiting had a definite architectural focus, with ten or twelve days spent in Venice and the surrounding area looking specifically at buildings by Palladio, annotating his copy of the *Quattro libri* as he went. Even more important for the future, he was able to purchase a number of architectural drawings by Palladio, including his studies of the great Roman bath complexes, and, on his return to London, two further

Jonathan Richardson, Portrait of Richard Boyle, third Earl of Burlington, *painted in 1719, the year of his second visit to Italy*

Inigo Jones, Design for a chimneypiece with alternative overmantels, *used by Burlington as a source for the Blue Velvet Room and Gallery*

ANDREA PALLADIO AND INIGO JONES

Palladio (1508–80), who was born in Padua, northern Italy, was possibly the most influential single figure in the history of Western architecture. He began his career by winning a competition to remodel the Basilica in Vicenza, and this led to a whole succession of commissions. His approach to design was based on a close study of ancient Roman remains, from which he derived his theories about ideal proportions. These were published in 1570 in his *I Quattro libri dell'architettura (The Four Books of Architecture)*, along with his designs for palaces, villas and churches, and his reconstructions of the ruins he had seen in Rome. Through this medium his influence spread in time throughout Europe and the British colonies in America. One of his earliest admirers was the English architect Inigo Jones (1573–1652) who, like Burlington, owned original drawings by Palladio and paid two formative visits to Italy. During the second of these, in 1613–14, he made a point of studying Palladio's buildings at first hand, annotating his copy of the *Quattro libri* as he went. This fired him with a missionary zeal to introduce what he felt were the most correct forms of classicism to England, something which his position as Surveyor of the King's Works to James I and then Charles I enabled him to do. His royal projects such as the Queen's House at Greenwich (begun in 1616) and the Banqueting House in Whitehall (begun in 1619) had a lasting effect on the course of English architecture, although their full potential was not realised until Lord Burlington's Palladian revival of a century later.

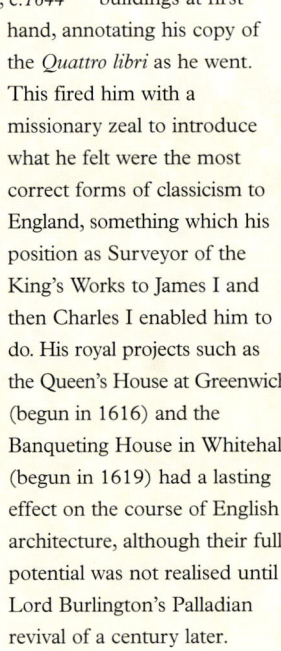

William Dobson, Portrait of Inigo Jones, *c.1644*

collections of drawings by Palladio and Inigo Jones. Together with his rapidly growing collection of books on the architecture of the Renaissance and Roman antiquity, these were to provide the main source of Burlington's inspiration as a budding designer. Indeed, the more he studied them, the less convinced he became that Campbell was a true follower of his new idols. It is likely that around 1720 Campbell produced a design for a new villa at Chiswick, based on Palladio's Villa Rotonda at Vicenza, with its four porticoes and crowning dome. Burlington, however, had already decided that the only way to get the results he wanted was to be his own architect.

The other great trophy which Burlington brought back from his second Italian tour was William Kent, whom he had already met on his earlier visit to Rome. Kent had been in Italy since 1709, sent there at the expense of a group of English gentlemen to train as a painter, and he returned to England so thoroughly imbued with Italian ways that in the Burlington household he was fondly referred to as the 'Signor'. Although it was in eighteenth-century terms a very unlikely friendship – the formal, reserved aristocrat and the ebullient, boozy, irreverent Yorkshireman – the two formed a close, lifelong association; so close that Kent henceforward treated Burlington House as his home, and was buried in the Burlington family vault at Chiswick parish church.

By 1720 the earl had soared to prominence as England's leading cultural arbiter, and he used his enormous influence to get his new friend openings as a painter, and then to insinuate him into a succession of increasingly important posts in the Office of Works. By this time it was Burlington's ambition to steer England away from the Baroque style, and to convert the country to the truer neo-Palladian faith. He realised he could not achieve this single-handed, especially since, as an aristocrat, he could not abandon his other responsibilities to pursue a full-time architectural career. As the realisation dawned that Kent would never be a great painter, so Burlington saw that his emerging genius as an architect and designer of interiors, furniture and gardens could be harnessed to the same ends. And so it was that, in the words of Horace Walpole, Lord Burlington became England's 'Apollo of the Arts', and William Kent 'his proper priest'.

Early Work at Chiswick

Before Kent appeared on the scene, Burlington had already been carrying out major works at Chiswick to remodel and extend the gardens attached to

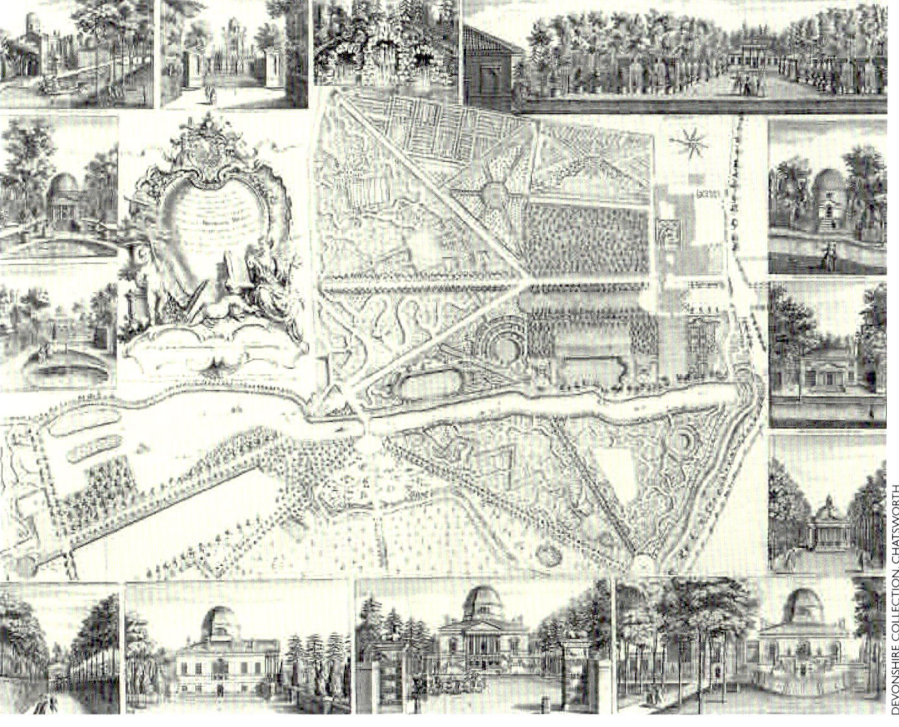

John Rocque, Plan of the Grounds at Chiswick, *1736, with vignettes showing the villa and the various garden buildings*

History of the House

Sculpture lining the edges of the Exedra

William Kent, First design for the Exedra, *subsequently reused by him as the Temple of British Worthies at Stowe House, Buckinghamshire*

the Jacobean house. This work might have begun as early as 1714, given that he was praised in print that year for his taste in gardening, but certainly it was well under way by 1717, the date of the Bagnio designed by Burlington to terminate one of the arms of the 'patte d'oie'. The early alterations were still very much in an existing formal tradition, and it is not known whether Burlington called in an established designer such as Charles Bridgeman, or whether he worked out his own layout. The proliferation in a relatively constricted area of a number of seemingly unrelated elements – the 'patte d'oie', the thickly planted Grove, the Orange Tree Garden and the two formal pools along the western edge of the site – may point to the latter.

Precise dating of both garden works and building works at Chiswick is often difficult, due to the scarcity of detailed accounts and absence of any written comments by Burlington, and has to be attempted with the help of a few dated paintings and engravings and of occasional references by visitors. Two things, however, are apparent. Firstly, it seems unlikely that Burlington ever had a clear 'master' plan for the grounds (which in any case doubled in size when further land was bought in 1726–7). Secondly, the layout was in a semi-continuous state of evolution from around 1715 until money ran out in the late 1730s. It is likely that the crucial role of William Kent was to interest the earl in his new ideas on garden design, involving the application of a more naturalistic and 'pictorial' approach. Chiswick was certainly one of the first places where he had an opportunity to put this into effect, which in practice meant removing or softening the divisions between existing compartments, and opening up space and views around the new villa.

The Construction of the New House

It is not known exactly when Burlington began to contemplate building a new house at Chiswick, although his thoughts were probably concentrated by a fire in 1725 which gutted the west wing of the Jacobean house. A letter of 1726 refers to the digging of foundations, and the following year Kent published the designs for the whole building nearly as it was executed. The date 1729 on the Red Velvet Room overmantels probably marks the effective completion of fitting out the interior. Historians have analysed the sources of the design, both inside and out, in great detail, and have concluded that although there are certainly many features culled from the original drawings by Palladio and Jones that Burlington owned, there are just as many derived from Roman antiquity. Indeed, though Burlington placed statues of Palladio and Jones on either side of the entrance, one of his main aims in architectural terms seems to have been to evoke the villas of ancient Rome as authentically as possible, for example in the ceiling of the Upper Link Room (see page 18) and in the coffering on the vault of the Tribunal (see page 8).

Even while building work was in progress, visitors commented on the main enigma about the villa: how was it intended to be used? Other villas then being built around London, however full of erudite references, came fully equipped with such conveniences as bedrooms and kitchens. (Marble Hill at Twickenham, also in the care of English Heritage, is a good example.) However, Sir John Clerk called Chiswick 'rather curious than convenient', while Lord Hervey wittily described it as being too small to live in, but too large to hang on a watch chain. In 1735 the young Duke of Cumberland, the future victor of the Battle of Culloden, dismissed it

---

THAMES-SIDE VILLAS

From the early seventeenth century onwards rich Londoners began to build themselves secondary residences around the fringes of the capital, intended primarily for summer holidays or retirement. Every village or hamlet acquired such houses, but those most favoured were along the Thames to the west, upwind of the city's smoke and dirt and accessible by boat. The trend was boosted by successive monarchs, who liked to spend time at their palaces at Richmond and Hampton Court, so that it became politically and socially desirable for courtiers and hangers-on to have a residence in the vicinity. In their function these houses resembled the villas created for the popes, cardinals and princes of the Italian Renaissance, and both Inigo Jones and Lord Burlington encouraged English clients and architects to give them an appropriate Italian form, inspired in particular by those designed by Andrea Palladio. By the mid-eighteenth century the banks of the Thames were lined with elegant residences in garden settings, such as Marble Hill House at Twickenham, generating a lively and relatively informal social scene, especially in centres such as Richmond and Twickenham.

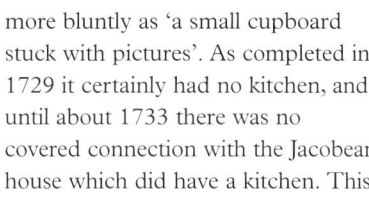

Marble Hill House, Twickenham

---

more bluntly as 'a small cupboard stuck with pictures'. As completed in 1729 it certainly had no kitchen, and until about 1733 there was no covered connection with the Jacobean house which did have a kitchen. This question of function is complicated by the fact that the earliest surviving inventory of contents is dated 1770, seventeen years after Burlington's death and twelve years after that of his wife. She certainly died in what is now called the Bedchamber on the first floor, but this does not necessarily prove that it was used as such in Burlington's time. Equally, the presence of beds in certain ground-floor rooms in 1770 does not mean that they had always been there. As for eating, food could have been carried through the Link Building after 1733, but in 1760 Horace Walpole noted that dining in fact took place in the old house.

The Purpose of Chiswick

The traditional interpretation of Chiswick House is that Burlington conceived it as an exquisite temple of the Arts, where he kept his most precious paintings, drawings and books and entertained selected friends. There is no doubt that in practice this is how it functioned, and the impression is confirmed by Rysbrack's paintings of the gardens in their early years, populated by busy gardeners, exotic birds and elegantly dressed guests enjoying themselves strolling, boating or fishing. Recently, however, a number of scholars have suggested that in fact there is much more to the villa – and indeed to Burlington himself – than meets the eye. It has been suggested firstly that the design and decoration are so full of masonic symbolism that the house could have been intended as a masonic temple, and secondly that there are various features reflecting strong but previously unsuspected Jacobite sympathies on Burlington's part.

Pieter Andreas Rysbrack, A View of Chiswick Gardens towards the Rear of the Bagnio, c.*1728–9*

As for the first of these suggestions, both Burlington and Kent have long been known to have been freemasons. They are listed in the *Freemason's Pocket Companion* of 1736, and it is possible that the earl might have become a member of the Grand Lodge soon after its formation in 1717. Freemasonry was certainly quite common among the English aristocracy and gentry of the early eighteenth century. Other well-known estates where masonic symbolism has been detected include Holkham Hall, Stourhead and West Wycombe. The alternative interpretation of the ceiling that Kent painted in the Red Velvet Room is interesting and plausible (see page 12). However, one difficulty with the idea that the villa is permeated with such double meanings is that many masonic symbols (for instance those associated with architecture) can also be read in a more straightforward way. Moreover, the argument that not only the rooms of the house but also the entire garden and its various structures formed an enormous integrated setting for masonic rituals is perhaps one that the modern visitor may find a little far-fetched. Indeed, given the lack of documentation, it seems likely that it can never be proved one way or the other.

The same is equally true of the second new interpretation. As early as 1713, Burlington was described by a contemporary as 'a good-natured pretty gentleman, but in Whig hands', so he was seemingly already considered a firm supporter of the Whig political party that was to come into its own with the arrival of the Hanoverian dynasty the following year. During George I's reign and the early years of George II's, he accumulated a number

Some of the original furniture from the Summer Parlour, now at Chatsworth House

Pieter Andreas Rysbrack, Chiswick House, the Pond and Temple, c.1729–31

Jacques Rigaud, The House Seen from the North-west, *1733. Much of the thickly planted Grove to the left was soon to be cut down to create the Exedra. The railings and hedges were also removed, probably on the advice of William Kent*

of official appointments that seem to reflect not just his exalted status and wealth but also his support for the king and government. But in May 1733 he suddenly resigned from every one of them and retired completely from Court life, apparently out of pique that George II, having promised him a lucrative new appointment, gave it instead to the third Duke of Devonshire. Some historians have argued that, despite having hitherto been to all appearances a loyal supporter of the Hanoverians, and of successive Whig governments under Sir Robert Walpole, Burlington was secretly an active supporter of the Tory opposition and of the Jacobites who wanted to see the return of the exiled Stuart 'king' James III, or 'the Old Pretender' as he was alternatively known. More than this, he was one of James's most important supporters, sending him large donations through a network of spies and intermediaries (some of them the foreign singers and musicians whom he imported to London) and running up substantial debts in the 1720s and 1730s. According to this fascinating but controversial theory, Chiswick can also be seen as a symbolic temple to the hoped-for return of the Stuart dynasty, as well as a masonic meeting place.

Whatever the true meaning of the Chiswick imagery, the creation of this complex and carefully considered work of architecture and horticulture must have absorbed a good deal of Burlington's time and money for the twenty or so years after about 1715. Moreover, there is evidence that, towards the end of this period, serious financial problems were probably dictating a halt to any further work. In around 1733, at about the same time that he withdrew from public life, he also seems to have largely withdrawn from the actual designing of buildings, having produced a relatively small but very influential corpus of works, and having advised on many more. Meanwhile he had established himself as the leading arbiter of architectural taste in Britain, and through this had been championing the work of Palladio. He must have felt that the torch had been successfully passed to his protégés, including William Kent, Henry Flitcroft and Isaac Ware, who had been placed in the most important official jobs and were creaming off some of the biggest and best commissions in the country.

The End of an Era

Burlington died on 4 December 1753 and was buried in the family vault on his Yorkshire estate at Londesborough. Lady Burlington survived him by five years. She was a strong and interesting character in her own right, who shared his cultural interests. Indeed, she had been taught to draw and paint by Kent and might have contributed ideas to the design of the house and gardens. Her temper, however, seems to have been rather uncertain and grew more so in her last years. Lord Hervey, who disliked both Burlingtons, called her 'Dame Palladio, insolent and bold, like her own chairman, whistle stamp and scold'. When she died in 1758 within a few days of Lady Bath, Horace Walpole mischievously speculated to a friend on her arrival at the Heavenly Gates: 'You know that the wife of Bath is gone to maunder at St Peter, and before he could hobble to the gate my Lady Burlington, cursing and blaspheming, overtook t'other Countess, and both together made such an uproar that…St Peter himself turned the key and hid himself.' She was predeceased by both her daughters, the younger of whom, Lady Charlotte Boyle, had married the Marquess of Hartington, the future fourth Duke of Devonshire. Thus it was that all the Burlington estates, properties and art collections came into the ownership of the Devonshire family, which is why today most of the items once at Chiswick are now at Chatsworth.

Jean Baptiste Van Loo, Lord and Lady Burlington with their Daughters and Black Servant, James Cambridge, *1739*

William Kent, Drawing of Lady Burlington's Flower Garden. *Lady Burlington and James Cambridge are shown gardening*

Chiswick under the fifth Duke of Devonshire

Charlotte's son, the fifth Duke, initiated changes that were to have a major impact on the appearance of both house and grounds. One of his first interventions in 1774 was to replace the wooden bridge over the river with an elegant stone structure, possibly designed by James Wyatt. In 1788 he decided to remedy the impractical arrangements bequeathed by his grandfather, demolishing the old Jacobean house and employing a little-known builder, surveyor and architect called John White to add substantial wings to the villa. Tactful though they were in design, Chiswick thereby ceased to be a villa and became instead a substantial mansion. In the gardens the duke began the process (completed by his son in the next century) of deformalising Burlington's layout, with advice from Capability Brown's successor Samuel Lapidge. In particular the Bagnio and Pagan Temple were demolished, and the 'patte d'oie' which had been such a key feature of the original design was effectively planted out. It was during this period that the duke's beautiful but controversial wife Georgiana (née Spencer) – celebrated in her time as a fashion icon but notorious for, amongst other things, her extramarital affairs and gambling debts – spent more and more of her time at Chiswick, which she called 'my earthly paradise'. She threw many lavish parties at Chiswick for her friends in the Whig party, and indeed soon after her death in 1806 the radical Whig politician Charles James Fox, with whom she had spent many hours at Chiswick, died in the house.

Photograph of Chiswick House in 1926, with the wings added in 1788 and demolished in the 1950s

Chiswick under the sixth Duke of Devonshire

Georgiana's son, the 'Bachelor' sixth Duke, also spent long periods at Chiswick, where he extended the grounds by purchasing the adjoining property to the east and creating an Italian Garden there. He too gave lavish parties, but these were more in the nature of semi-official receptions than party-political events, and certainly completely different from Burlington's select artistic gatherings. In 1814 he played host to European leaders in London for premature celebrations of what was thought to be the end of the Napoleonic Wars, including the Russian Tsar and the King of Prussia. An even grander occasion was the party for Tsar Nicholas I in 1844, attended by Prince Albert, the King of Saxony, and about 700 members of the British nobility – 'one of the most splendid fêtes ever celebrated in this or any other country', claimed the *London Illustrated News*. Like his mother, the Bachelor Duke was a keen gardener, and he also introduced a selection of exotic animals, including an elephant, elks, emus, kangaroos, an Indian bull and cow and a Neapolitan pig. For the party in 1844 there were several giraffes on display with their Egyptian keepers, en route from Surrey Zoological Gardens to St Petersburg.

Reception for Tsar Nicholas I from the Illustrated London News, *15 June 1844*

Chiswick in the Late Nineteenth Century

After the duke's death in 1858 his sister lived on at Chiswick for a few more years, but thereafter the house was let to a succession of tenants. These were mostly grand or very grand, including in 1870 the Prince of Wales and, from 1881 to 1892, the Marquess of Bute. But after Bute's departure the tenant until 1929 was a private mental institution; Chiswick's decline from aristocratic grandeur had begun. In 1929 the ninth Duke sold the estate to Middlesex County Council in the hope of safeguarding it from future development (the park had already been sold off for development by the seventh Duke in 1884). Vested in the care of the Borough of Brentford and Chiswick, the condition of the house in

This watercolour by William Hunt shows the Gallery as it was in 1828, with the gilded side tables, Kent chairs and porphyry urns still in place

The café in one of the wings, photographed in 1947

particular deteriorated seriously, even though some repair work continued until 1941. Eventually in 1948, prompted by concern from Queen Mary and the Georgian Group, the house was handed over to the Ministry of Works.

Recent History

The restoration campaign of the 1950s began in the garden, where in 1951–2 a laudable attempt was made to recreate the 'patte d'oie' behind the house in something like its original form. Attitudes to Chiswick were indeed very much dominated by a feeling that it was the Burlington phase which really mattered, and when attention turned to the house the decision was taken that it too should be returned to its original design. This is probably not a decision which would now be taken so readily, if at all, but the poor condition of the wings, riddled with every kind of rot, made it easier to opt for demolition in 1956–7. In the process the side elevations of the villa, invisible since 1788, were recreated, along with the obelisk chimneys that had been replaced as early as the 1730s, and the Link Building re-emerged from inside the late-Georgian casing of the east wing. Within, the main rooms were restored as far as possible to how it was thought they appeared in Burlington's day, given the constraints of funding and available information, and the absence of original contents due to their migration to Chatsworth. In 1984 responsibility for the house was transferred to the newly formed English Heritage, which has continued this policy, while the grounds remain the responsibility of the local borough council.

Further Reading

Toby Barnard and Jane Clark (eds), *Lord Burlington: Architecture, Art and Life* (London, 1995)

Julius Bryant, 'Chiswick House – The Inside Story', *Apollo*, CXXXVI (1992), pp.17–22

Julius Bryant, *London's Country House Collections* (London, 1993)

Julius Bryant, 'The Refurnishing of Chiswick House', *The Georgian Group Journal* (1995), pp.103–6

Jacques Carré, *Lord Burlington (1694–1753), le connaisseur, le mécène, l'architecte* (1993)

Edward Corp (ed.), *Lord Burlington: The Man and his Politics* (Lewiston, NY, 1998)

John Harris, *The Palladian Revival: Lord Burlington, His Villa and Garden at Chiswick* (New Haven and London, 1994)

Richard Hewlings, 'The Link Room at Chiswick House', *Apollo*, CXLI (1995), pp.28–9

Treve Rosoman, 'The Decoration and Use of the Principal Apartments of Chiswick House, 1727–70', *Burlington Magazine*, CXXVII (1985), pp.663–77

Treve Rosoman, 'The Chiswick House Inventory of 1770', *Furniture History*, XXII (1986), pp.81–102

R.T. Spence, 'Chiswick House and its gardens, 1726–1732', *Burlington Magazine*, CXXXV (1993), pp.525–31